MEMORIES
OF OLD
YORKSHIRE

AURORA PUBLISHING.

First published in Great Britain in 1994 by
Aurora Publishing
Unit 9 Bradley Fold Trading Estate
Radcliffe Moor Road, Bradley Fold
Bolton, Lancashire BL2 6RT

ISBN 1 85926 046 2 Hardback
ISBN 1 85926 048 9 Paperback

Produced by
PDH Book Print Production
Castleton, Rochdale OL11 2XD

Printed in Italy by:
- Tipografia Umbra -
Città di Castello

*Our sincere thanks to Mr. Tom Heavyside for allowing us to use his excellent photographs which we
have included in the industrial section of this book.*

CONTENTS

YORKSHIRE

Yorkshire, rightly, has a reputation for hauntingly beautiful scenery, from the softer beauty of the Dales to the more rugged, vast uninterrupted expanses of moorland. The area has been subjected to all sorts of early foreign invasion: the Celts, the Romans, the Anglo-Saxons, the Normans and the Vikings. It still bears many of the remains of these invasions, and we have some splendid castles, roads, place names and relics as a result. The Dales and the Moors comprise two of the country's National Parks in one county, and offer varied and breath-taking scenery. It is easy to imagine the setting of Emily Brontë's ``Wuthering Heights'' and the eerie magic of the tale when in the midst of the moors of Yorkshire.

Yorkshire is a county fortunate to have attractive and varied coastline, too. Bordering the North Sea, which has been the scene of many shipwrecks and brave deeds, the coast is prone to erosion, such as the dramatic cliff fall in Scarborough in recent times. Whitby is perhaps one of the most attractive of the seaside towns, and nearby Robin Hood's Bay is a photo opportunity which few can resist. However, Yorkshire is not all rural and coastal. It has a number of large towns and cities including the spa town of Harrogate, known for its elegance, the university town of Leeds, and the industrial towns which were at the heart of the woollen industry, Bradford and Halifax. These conurbations contain some splendid buildings, symbolic of the wealth of the area during the Industrial Revolution.

TOWNS AND CITIES

Yorkshire is a large region encompassing the counties of West, South and North Yorkshire which replaced the Old Ridings. It therefore contains numerous towns and large cities, varying in character. Many of these developed with the industrial revolution, using the wealth of the wool and coal industries to build their civic centres and provide local amenities. The cities form a curious mixture from the more historically interesting tourist attractions, such as York and the spa town of Harrogate to the north, to the industrial and commercial centres such as Leeds, Bradford and Sheffield to the west and south. Some of these centres were home to legends such as Titus Salt, who developed the fascinating model village of Saltaire for workers at his mill in Bradford, and of course, Marks and Spencer, who set up their now vast enterprise from the humble beginnings of a trestle table in Kirkgate Market, Leeds in 1884. Certain centres developed expertise in creating specific products – Sheffield, for example, was once synonymous with the production of steel. As traditional industries have waned, the characters of the larger towns and cities have changed, but the Yorkshire people have met the challenges once again with many areas continuing to develop both commercially and academically.

The Royal Pump Room, Harrogate. c. 1923

The Royal Pump Room is now a museum of local history in this inland spa town, but it is still possible to take the healing waters within the museum. Harrogate is one of the most elegant towns in the country with its Victorian and Edwardian buildings, and is certainly the most sophisticated centre of Yorkshire.

Boar Lane, Leeds. c. 1907

Boar Lane was and is one of the main shopping streets of Leeds, as this photograph illustrates. The hustle and bustle are indicative of the importance of Leeds as a major Yorkshire commercial centre.

Parliament Street, Harrogate. c. 1912

Harrogate was considered a holiday resort for smart people until the 1930s. No longer a holiday resort, it is still considered a very civilised and attractive town, with a fascinating array of shops, tea shops and heritage.

York Minster and City Wall. c. 1903

The Minster appears in the skyline from almost every direction in York and is a magnificent and imposing building. It is of the early English to perpendicular period and is particularly famous for its west front and towers. The central tower suffered devastation in 1984 when it was struck by lightning, and needed four years worth of work to repair the damage. The Minster, for all its beauty, seems dogged by disaster. In 1829, a man named Jonathan Martin, said to have been suffering from 'acute mania' concealed himself and set fire to the choir causing damage to the oak, organ, roof, pulpit and stalls, with damage of £65,000. Martin was committed to an asylum.

Another serious fire in 1840 ruined the south-west tower and the roof of the Nave. Despite its problems, York remains dominated by its Minster, regardless of the array of equally ancient buildings around it.

After the Fire, Selby Abbey. 1906

The photograph is not the clearest but is included for its historical
interest. The abbey church is of late-Norman to perpendicular period
and was partly destroyed by fire in 1906. However, it was restored
following this. The abbey had another disaster befall it when the
central tower collapsed in 1690. It was said to be founded in 1069 by a
runaway French monk, who brought with him a stolen finger of St.
Germain of Auxerre. The style of abbey evolved over 250 years of
building, and the building itself is a wonder for such a small town as
Selby.

Draper's Shop, Leeds. c. 1926

A rather solid-looking and fancy corner shop building in Leeds, crammed to the brim with goods for sale. Corner shops tend mainly to be of newsagent and grocer variety these days, but the 1920s saw a number of specialist outlets such as the one pictured here. Photographs like this, with the proprietor standing proudly outside were common. This would be a stopping place for a measure of cloth, carpet and linoleum, hosiery and shirts, caps and other items of gents' clothing wear. The window display looks as if it would take hours of work. Shops were, in many ways, very attractive with their variety, and the hand-painted signs, rather different from the chains of shops today which make many towns indistinguishable from each other.

Petergate, York. c. 1917

York is *the* tourist attraction for the region. Every year, visitors flock
to the city which was invaded by the Romans, and the Vikings, and
which was later developed by the church, the medieval guilds, the
Georgians, the chocolate manufacturers and the advent of the
railways. The city is both attractive and historically fascinating with
more than its fair share of churches, castles, museums, interesting
shops and walkways, plus of course, the city wall and the river.

High Street, Pateley Bridge. c. 1926

Near to Harrogate in the area of Nidderdale lies the attractive village of Pateley Bridge, with its extensive views of the Dales. Pately Bridge has developed into a popular stopping place for walkers who are visiting Nidderdale. The town is noted for its friendly, hospitable atmosphere. The town is known to locals for its old church, St. Mary's, which contains many tombstones and memorials – one of particular interest is that of Mary Myers, a local woman who died aged nearly 120 in 1743, a remarkable age even by modern standards.

Cleckheaton Public Library, 1954

North Street, Ripon

Ripon is a cathedral city dating from 886AD. Other attractions are numerous including a Police and Prison Museum, a market and a race course.

The Kursaal, Harrogate. c. 1920

At this time, the location of a recital and obviously a popular place.
This picture dates from the times when Harrogate was still a highly
fashionable resort, where many people visited not only to take the
waters, but to enjoy the many pleasures the town had to offer. At this
time it was a town of magnificent hotels, pavilions, concert rooms
and promenades – indeed, changes in this sense have been few.
Earlier this century, the theatre was visited by many of the best actors
and actresses of the day, and the town was rapidly becoming known
for its concerts.

Bootham Bar, York. c.1910

Bar is simply another word for gate. York has four of these – Bootham Bar, Micklegate Bar, Monk Bar, and Walmgate. Obviously, where there is a city wall, there are also bars. Bootham Bar, with its portcullis is situated west of the Minster and is the gateway to the north. Its barbican was said to have been the finest in York but was taken down in 1831. The vaulted rooms of the bars would contain warders and keepers who were particularly important in times of war or invasion. On a more gruesome note, it would generally be the bars where heads were displayed on pikes for all to see during battle. The narrow gateways would have been the scene of many military clashes.

Shambles, York. c. 1914

One of the oldest streets in York is the narrow Shambles. This was a centre for the butcher's trade, but now must surely be one of the most photographed streets in the city, with its attractive buildings.

Knaresborough. c. 1930

A popular view of Knaresborough with the bridge and the river
providing an enjoyable day out. Knaresborough, for some reason, has
a number of associations with eccentrics. Mother Shipton and the
dripping well are well known. Less famous is Blind Jack, a man who
suffered smallpox which led to blindness at the age of six. This
disability seemed to mean nothing to him – he became an expert
swimmer, practised the violin for a living, went hunting and had an
extraordinary ability to find his way around. However, his most
serious business was making highways and roads, showing great
engineering skills. The town has quite a history. Oliver Cromwell
once lodged here, and Dr. Stubbs (once Bishop of Oxford) and
William Kaye the scholar were both born here.

City Square, Leeds. c. 1918

Leeds is a university city which is a curious mixture of modern developments and old buildings. City Square, near to the railway station and The Queen's hotel hasn't changed too much and is recognisable from this picture. City Square forms the centre point of the city and used to be known as Victoria Square. The Square is close to the railway station which became an important aspect of the city's industrial success.

Modern re-development of the centre belies the fact that Leeds is one of the most ancient centres in the northern shires – it was a Roman Station and existed during the time of Edward the Confessor according to the Domesday Book.

Kirkgate, Bradford. c. 1919

A busy cobbled street in this post World War I picture.

Skipton High Street and Cenotaph. c. 1928

Skipton is an interesting town situated on the Aire, picturesque with its wide streets, and famous for its cattle markets. It was a centre for the spinning and weaving of cotton, but also a large agricultural trading centre. However, it never reached the commercial importance of Leeds or Bradford.

Briggate, Leeds. c. 1928

Another main street with some high grade shops and hotels. Briggate
is an ancient street with the advantage of space. It once held the cloth
market and contained several old burgage houses. Near to the Moot
Hall, with its pillory and stocks was a market cross and alms-houses.
This has, of course, all changed now and the street is of more interest
to shoppers than to historians.

Duncan Street, Leeds. c. 1909

Leeds was and is a fine commercial centre with many shopping
streets like this.

York Minister, West Front

The West Front is the most famous view of York Minster which is the largest medieval cathedral in Northern Europe, with splendid towers and stained glass windows.

HAWORTH AND THE BRONTËS

The somewhat bleak village of Haworth situated on the edge of rugged moorland is renowned for its Brontë associations (indeed it has based its prosperity on this literary connection). Now, it is quite a tourist attraction. The village Main Street is a steep incline which is usually very busy these days with tourists and shops.
There is little left of the Haworth which the Brontës would have known except the great moorland beyond the village. The old church was rebuilt in 1880 and the parsonage has also changed. However, the shrine to the literary sisters remains an attraction to visitors seeking insight into the lives of these astonishing women.

"Wuthering Heights", Top Withens, Haworth. c.1918

Reputedly the Brontë sisters' (Anne, Emily and Charlotte) favourite walk was the two miles to a small waterfall, now of course known as the Brontë Falls – the route is signposted from the top of the village. Approximately one mile further is the site of the farmhouse ruin called Top Withens which is said to be the setting for "Wuthering Heights", the home of the Earnshaw family. Certainly, the moorland setting is appropriate even if it wasn't the building that Emily Brontë used in her novel. The idea remains popular and thousands of tourists make the trek to see this desolate building as a result.

Brontë Old Parsonage

The parsonage was once the home of the literary Brontë family which is now cared for by the Brontë Society. The rooms are still furnished as in the Brontës' day and contain personal items, books, manuscripts and pictures. Reverend Brontë moved to the parsonage in 1820 with his wife and family. The place would then have had a rigorous climate and a barely civilized population. It must have been difficult for the family when Mrs. Brontë died in 1821 from consumption leaving her children without a mother.

In the cemetery is the grave of Lily Cove Britain's first balloonist and parachutist who died during a performance in 1911. Every member of the Brontë family were also interred here except for Anne who died and was buried in Scarborough.

Charlotte Brontë (1816–55)

Perhaps the most famous of the Brontë sisters, Charlotte, the writer of "Jane Eyre" died in her thirties during pregnancy, having married her father's curate. It appears that she may have died of the pregnancy disease, eclampsia. Her sisters died at the ages of 29 (Anne) and 30 (Emily) both from tuberculosis, and her brother Bramwell at 31 from alcohol and opium addition. A talented but sadly blighted family.

Reverend Brontë (1777–1861)

Father to the talented offspring. The Reverend was thought to be a fairly solitary figure living in the isolated Parsonage. It is perhaps partly the peculiar upbringing of his children that nurtured their imaginations and fostered their talents. He outlived all his children.

Post Office and Stocks, Haworth. c. 1928

Main Street, Haworth. c. 1930

Brontë Museum, Haworth

The museum houses drawings, paintings and miniature books, Charlotte's letters to friends and her writing desk, and the surviving possessions of the enigmatic Emily who died at the age of 30. The rooms are restored to their appearance as in the early 1850s.

The Brontë family were unusual by any standards. Patrick Brontë was said to be quietly strong, determined and resolved, and probably had to be to raise his children alone. His work must have been difficult as he was a staunch Tory churchman in a parish of Radicals and Dissenters. Bramwell was in some ways the saddest member of the family, whose talents were wasted in a world of alcohol and drugs. The Museum is worth a visit to see the belongings of the sisters, but it seemed to be the environment which was of greater importance with Emily fascinated by the wild moors, Anne delighted by the distance and horizon, and the buildings of great interest to Charlotte.

MARKET DAYS AND TOWNS

Market Towns are those granted a borough charter to hold a weekly market; many were created during 1100–1200 when such charters were sold to bring in revenue to the Crown.
The market square enabled the easy collection of tolls. Such towns flourished in the Middle Ages and their prosperity is often marked by elegant buildings and statues in the Market Square. Today, the only important local markets are those dealing in livestock although many towns still use their market squares for trading.

Market Square, Knaresborough. c. 1933

Knaresborough is a picturesque Yorkshire market town with an excellent placing on the River Nidd. The Market Place is said to have the oldest chemist's shop in England, dating from 1720, where special recipe lavender water is still obtainable. The town is also of course known for the legend of Old Mother Shipton and the Petrifying Well, and in more modern times, the annual Bed Race, which is a bed push for charity around the town, including a river crossing.

Bull Ring, Wakefield. c. 1908

A busy photograph with numerous horses and carriages waiting.

Market Place, Hawes. c. 1931

Hawes is unremarkable in itself, indeed little more than a straggling one-street stone village, but its situation is magnificent, nestled among some of England's finest scenery in Yorkshire's picturesque Wensleydale and it is seen as the capital of the area. Nearby are Semer Water, thought to be one of the country's most beautiful reservoirs and the waterfall at Hardraw Force.

Hawes is said to be the highest market-town in the country being about 800 feet above sea level. From a distance it is more imposing than at close quarters. It was probably at its most characteristic on market day or during a sheep-fair when thousands of sheep would be driven in from all sides. What the town itself lacks is more than compensated for by the romantic and picturesque surroundings, especially Buttertubs Pass to Swaledale during snowfall.

Market Day, Selby. c. 1915

Market Place, Netherton

Market Day, Richmond. c. 1918

Home to the song the "Lass of Richmond Hill", this town is beautifully situated in Swaledale. The Market Place is one of the largest in the country, and picturesque. It is an open space, paved with cobble stones. In its centre stands the Trinity Church which is mixed in with shops and houses, rather curious for an ecclesiastical building. In the tower of the Church it became the custom from the time of William The Conqueror to toll the curfew bell at eight o'clock. The 18th century obelisk is also worthy of note. In medieval times, Richmond was a small walled town whose main trade was cattle and the manufacture of yarn stockings.

Market Place, Doncaster. c. 1914

Doncaster was once a market town noted for its large Market Hall set in an extensive square, which contained a Corn Exchange and Market, a Wool Market, a Cattle Market and Town Hall. The town became quite keen on the introduction of rules of conduct and bye-laws which gave it a reputation for cleanliness. Townsfolk were penalized if they did not clean the pavement in front of their houses at least three times a week, or if they allowed their pigs to run in the street.

Market Place, Masham. c. 1909

A strangely deserted Market Place. This is a huge site containing a church with a tower and spire. Masham itself consists mainly of the market square, surrounded by the old houses with an obelisk rising from four steps in the centre. The most interesting object is the parish church, partly because of its architecture especially the octagonal spire, but also because of its history. There were good markets and fairs in Masham in past times, especially of cattle and sheep, when open house was kept and visitors were treated to a dish of roast beef and pickled cabbage. Even then the town was generally quiet except on market days.

LEISURE

Yorkshire is famous for a number of things, among them cricket and brass bands. Not only do the people enjoy their leisure activities, they often also excel at them. There have been a number of notable, talented cricketers from the county and many areas have successful brass bands.

This is perhaps the most appropriate part of the book to mention the art of cooking. Yorkshire is renowned for its batter pudding made from eggs, milk, water and flour and served traditionally with roast beef. Eating good, plain food is something of a leisure activity in the region – the pudding is often served with gravy (or mint sauce) before the main course, a custom originally developed to take the edge off the family's appetite. However it is eaten, it is well worth a try.

Hallfield Baptist Cricket Club. c. 1912

Yorkshire is renowned for its love of cricket, and skill at the game. It has a long tradition of high class league. It is considered a sport enjoyed by all social classes and people of varying abilities – presumably this church group would have been less likely than most teams to enjoy the repartee at the bar afterwards!

In terms of county cricket, the county championship competition dates from 1864 and Yorkshire holds the record for most wins. Yorkshire has a long tradition of cricket leagues, generally amateur and many villages have their own teams and cricket clubs.

The Hornblower, Ripon. c. 1905

The Ripon Hornblower appears every evening at 9pm to blow his horn at the corner of the obelisk in Market Place. The ritual has taken place for over 100 years and was originally to assure the local citizens that they were safe for the night.

**Children's Corner, Scarborough.
c. 1909**

Most seaside resorts had a children's
corner which would have some sandy
beach and safe, shallow waters for the
children to play in.

Dripping Well, Knaresborough. 1936

The Petrifying Well is one of
Knaresborough's major attractions,
linked with the legend of the local
prophetess, old Mother Shipton who
was rumoured to have lived in the
Cave near to the well.

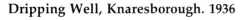

Board School, Intake. c. 1916

The School Boards ran elementary schools prior to the establishment of the Local Education Authorities. A rather austere looking building here but unlike their earlier counterparts, the children were fortunate to have some degree of basic education. While education is hardly considered a leisure activity today, it must have compared favourably to the previous existence of many children.

The 1870 Education Act marked the first attempt at widespread provision of State elementary education but it was not really until the 1944 Education Act that free, universal secondary education was introduced and that controls on standards were applied.

Thornton's Tea Rooms, Hardcastle Crags. c. 1917

The idea of afternoon tea (taken from 4–5pm) was devised during the mid 17th century to bridge the gap between lunch and dinner which would normally take place at around 8pm. The beverage itself is said to have been brought to Europe by the Dutch in the 17th century, although there are records of earlier tea drinking in Britain. Tea itself rapidly became the great British beverage and Yorkshire is thought to be one of the key tea-drinking areas.

Brighouse and Rastrick Band. 1929

This famous band were Belle Vue champions in 1929. Belle Vue
commonly held competitions among brass bands. The band is still
popular today and even had a hit record which reached the charts.
This particular band won a number of prizes for their performances.

On the Wharfe, Ilkley. c. 1920

Ilkley is very high up, on the site of a Roman fort and is surrounded
by fine scenery. It stands by the River Wharfe. Ilkley is of course
famous to many because of the song ''Ilkley Moor B'aht 'at''.

The Five Locks, Leeds and Liverpool Canal, Bingley. c. 1922

This canal was part of the important 18th century canal network development. The 20th century saw a rapid decline in the canal system for trade purposes but there is still an interest in this feat of engineering and canals are now largely tourist attractions.

The canals took direct routes across the landscape and were considered in their day to be rapid and safe. Certainly, the Leeds and Liverpool Canal would originally have been one of the best ways of transporting heavy goods and manufactured products to the port of Liverpool. Roads across the Pennines would have been at worst impassable and at best unsurfaced.

Cowthorpe near Wetherby. c. 1907

Children at play. How serious and like young adults they look with their solemn faces, stances and clothing. The thatched roof is an unusual sight in the North of England.

Horse Shoe Pond, Doncaster. c. 1910

This was obviously a popular place for walking with the pram judging by the numbers of women out with their offspring. Doncaster itself was mainly associated with horse-racing with the famous St. Leger being popular in the area – the grandstand was built in 1776. It was said that the St. Leger meeting was the social event of the year in the north and that more families met each other at Doncaster races than anywhere else. The town's other claim to fame is production of butterscotch.

"Amos" Barnsley's Mascot. c. 1918

It is easy to feel a certain sympathy for this donkey "Amos" with his heavy and possibly less than sober burden outside the Clarence Hotel.

Royal Visit to Heckmondwike, May 30th, 1918

Security would be much tighter today for such a visit!
Heckmondwike lies in the Spen Valley area close to Batley and
Dewsbury which was a densely populated area of collieries, mills and
factories. It was an area known for the production of shoddy, a
mixture of wool with shreddings of old woollen and worsted rags.
No doubt the town was presented at its best for the royal visit.

RURAL LIFE

Yorkshire is fortunate in having more than its fair share of rural areas alongside the industrial and commercial centres. Many of the farming villages of the Dales and Moors are still primarily agricultural but are also tourist attractions. Despite the common notion of rural idyll, life in the country communities could be hard, with limited transport, and reliance on good prices for animals for a living. The weather in the country could be harsh and the hills, while scenic and picturesque for the traveller, could make life difficult for the farming families.

Brearton Village. c. 1914

A lively looking crowd, perhaps on their way to church given the
wearing of hats, in this small North Yorkshire village, situated
between Harrogate and Ripon.

Skipton Castle. c. 1914

The castle dates from the 11th century and is known for its yew tree planted by Lady Anne Clifford in 1659. The castle belonged to the powerful Clifford family. It is one of the best preserved castles of its time in England. Its round towers may be seen from this aerial photograph.

The towers are the oldest parts of the building with the semi-circular arch which forms the west door of the inner castle. Until relatively recent times, the people of Skipton were thought to be great believers in witchcraft and magic with the nearby "Witches' Hill" thought to be the site of unholy rites. There were numerous "wise men" of Skipton who helped local farmers with their problems. Those days are gone but the town is still a convenient point from which to tour Airedale.

Bolton Abbey. c. 1924

This 12th century abbey is situated on the River Wharfe which can be
crossed by the footbridge or the 57 stepping stones on the site, which
were generally used before the footbridge was built. The stones are
featured in this photograph and would require a steady foot to cross.

Grassington Square. c. 1910

Grassington is yet another charming North Yorkshire village with narrow streets and a small, cobbled square. Yorkshire seems to have been well-endowed with delightful rural villages.

Grassington was once the centre of many customs. One recreation was clock-dressing, where people met to dress the clock; another was stang riding which involved a cart instead of a pole, and no burning of effigies as was the rule in most Yorkshire villages. There was a curious funeral ceremony here – the coffin would be carried from the house and put on chairs before the door, with mourners gathered around. A key person would then announce a hymn, reciting the first verse. This was then sung slowly and solemnly, the coffin would be lifted, a procession formed and the hymn sung on the way to the graveyard.

A notorious murder occurred near to here – the perpetrator was arrested, tried and found guilty, then hung from a tree where the murder was committed, known to the locals as Dark Corner.

Ardsley Village Smithy, nr. Barnsley. c.1903

The village smithy was an essential part of village life. When horses were still quite widely used for transport, on farms and in industry the blacksmith was indispensable. As well as shoeing horses, he would often carry out repairs to farm equipment and some may even have sold items such as wheels for the carts. The blacksmith's would often be a meeting place for the local people where they could catch up on the latest news while their horse was being shod. Still an important skill these days although the horses are used in general for pleasure purposes rather than as for working animals.

Rural Scene, Holbeck, nr. Leeds. c. 1909

Malham Village and River Aire. c. 1917

Situated on the Pennine Way, Malham has spectacular limestone
cliffs and waterfalls at Gordale Scar. The limestone scenery is perhaps
some of the most striking in Yorkshire. Malham itself is little more
than a hamlet but is a very popular stopping place during the
summer.

Malham Cove, close to the village, is celebrated as being one of the
finest rock scenes in the world. It is a vast segment of a circle of
limestone rock, 285 feet in height. The head of the Cove offers
magnificent views of the surrounding moorland. The limestone is
part of a cliff known as the Craven Fault. Malham Tarn, a lake some
three miles in circumference is also worth a viewing.

THE COAST

Yorkshire has 114 miles of coastline which is a combination of cliffs, headlands, bays, beaches, and coves. There are a number of popular holiday resorts on this border with the North Sea, the largest of these being Scarborough. The coast is at its most interesting north of Scarborough, especially around Whitby and Robin Hood's Bay. In Fletcher's ''Picturesque History of Yorkshire'' (published 1901) the main resorts are described as follows:-

Scarborough – ''a Bank-Holidayish sort of place''.
Whitby – ''a somewhat stately and reserved place . . . favourite resort of artists, authors and Americans''.
Filey – ''an ideal refuge for young married couples, children in charge of governesses and quiet old ladies''.
Bridlington – ''by way of becoming a second Scarborough in regard to that nuisance, a cheaper tripper''.

Although somewhat tongue in cheek, today's visitors will draw their own conclusions when investigating the popular coastal resorts and the interesting places in between.

Peasholm Lake, Scarborough. c. 1940

A wonderful picture of rowers boating on the lake, circuiting the
bandstand seated on a parapet in the water. Within Peasholme Park it
is still possible to row round the island with its pagoda and waterfall.
The park has other attractions, such as fairy lights at night. It is
situated near the North Bay which is sandy and considered to be less
commercialized than the popular "Golden Nile" atmosphere of the
South Bay.

The Steps, East Cliff, Whitby. c. 1924

Looking at old photographs of seaside resorts, it is almost always the case that children are sitting with their summer clothes on and buckets and spades at the ready, while the parents look uncomfortably fully-clad. Presumably, the new freedoms of the 1920s had not yet arrived in Whitby.

Italian Terrace Spa, Scarborough. c. 1909

Scarborough became quite a popular resort perhaps because of its two sandy bays. Its popularity as a spa town dates from the 17th century, and in the 19th century, the railway development attracted many visitors.

One of the attractions of Scarborough is that it is situated on the Southern edge of the North Yorkshire Moors National Park, so the attractions of the seaside resort may be combined with the views from the hillsides, old villages, and moorland. Scarborough houses two bays and various parks, and gardens which are attractively laid out. For those interested in the Brontës, the grave of Anne Brontë is in the churchyard; she died in 1849. The Italian Gardens landscaped down the cliffside are at South Bay and add beauty to the area.

Bempton Cliff Climbers

The cliffs near Bempton are a home for England's largest seabird breeding colony and is now a site for the RSPB reserve at Bempton Cliffs. There are colonies of gannets, kittiwakes, herring gulls, guillemots, shags, puffins and other seabirds. This picture shows men collecting eggs from the cliffs.

For many years it was the custom of local people to descend the cliffs to collect bird eggs; this was known as 'cliff climbing'. Usually, four men were required to carry out the task, along with an iron wheel and a well-greased stout rope, plus leather straps used as a cradle. Care had to be taken to descend with one's back to the sea and there would be a drop of three to four hundred feet. Eggs would be gathered usually for collection purposes and professional 'climbers' would collect eggs to sell. From the cliffs the 'climbers' would be able to see thousands of birds.

The Harbour, Bridlington. c. 1920

Bridlington developed into a popular family resort offering fine
sands, sailing, fishing, safe bathing and the usual array of seaside
entertainments.

Bay Bank, Robin Hood's Bay. c. 1909

This picturesque village can only be approached on foot, and it is easy to see why when the steep hillside with its cluster of houses is espied. It was mainly a fishing village, but was not without its fair share of smuggling as was often the case with these inaccessible coastal villages.

   This small resort and fishing village is the most northern example of placenames given in honour of the English folk hero, Robin Hood. This is a typical scene and shows the scenic nature of the village.

New Quay, Whitby. c. 1911

Whitby is a fishing port and a seaside resort and has links with Captain Cook and whaling. Being on the treacherous North Sea coast, it also has a tradition of sea rescue and the Whitby lifeboatmen are renowned for their courage. Whitby is an area of historical importance with an abbey on the clifftop, standing stones, a trade in jet and excellent scenery to the west.

The town is divided into two parts – the Old Town on the east side and the modern on the West Cliff. During the last century, Whitby was an important herring fishing area – now pleasure craft mix with the fishing boats.

"Hispaniola" in Scarborough Harbour. c. 1929

Crowds flocking to see the old sailing ship still with the pirate's skull
and crossbones aloft. Presumably, this ship was meant to be a replica
of Hispaniola of Stevenson's "Treasure Island", where most of the
crew were cut-throat pirates looking for treasure.

Whitby Harbour. c. 1938

Whitby is known for its harbour at the mouth of the River Esk. A successful fishing and previously a whaling town, a whalebone archway presented by the whaling nation of Norway, overlooks the town.

Whitby was more important in the past than today in commercial terms. It was a great ship-building town, and was once ranked the seventh port in respect of tonnage. The hazardous occupation of whaling died out c.1840 and was replaced by curing fish, especially herrings. The oldest trade in the area not pertaining to the sea was the manufacture of jet ornaments. Today, the harbour is noted for its charm and beauty.

North Landing, Flamborough. c.1939

With a view of the fine chalk cliffs.

Covet Hill Steps, Robin Hood's Bay. c.1906

Filey Beach. c. 1912

Filey has superb beaches, and this picture captures the seaside fun in 1912 for a family group. They are sitting in the shelter of the cliffs on what can be a rather cold beach. The children have their spades but the adults are relaxing, breathing in the sea air with their hats and outerwear on.

Filey was once a small fishing village with a few hotels and boarding houses, but when this picture was taken it was an established resort. It is still a small and more select, quiet resort with excellent cliffs. Fishing is still an occupation for local people. Filey Brigg is a tremendous sight during stormy seas.

Flamborough, New Lighthouse. c. 1923

Once the site of a naval battle (1779), most of the attraction today revolves around nearby Flamborough Head which is known for its chalk cliffs and which was the scene of a successful invasion by the Vikings. The lighthouse standing near the sea is also made of chalk.

TRANSPORT AND INDUSTRY

Yorkshire encompasses hills, dales and moorland, coast, towns and cities and therefore is home to numerous industries. Transport developed in the area to enable the more efficient running of these industries. West and South Yorkshire contained the old wool and cloth mills and coal mines which were a key to the region's prosperity and civic development.

These old industries have now diminished and left pockets of unemployment in the region. North Yorkshire has tended, because of its landscape, to be better suited to rural industries, such as farming, and has used its natural attractions to encourage the growth of tourism which is an important development.

The coastal areas still, of course, rely on fishing to some extent, but again resorts have grown to attract people to the area during the Summer months. The advent of canals and later railways were of tremendous importance to the area for moving manufactured products and bringing in raw materials.

Barge on Canal, c. 1914

This Leeds Company owned barge is probably sited on the Leeds-Liverpool Canal in this picture, at a time when the canals were still used for some trades as a means of transport.

   The success of the Bridgewater canal, opened in 1761, to carry coal from the Worsley mines to Manchester, was the inspiration for the canal boom and new routes soon spread all over the country. After 1830 the expansion of the canals was dramatically slowed down by the introduction of the railways and in the 20th century the canals were hit still further due to the use of road haulage. Both of these new forms of transportation soon became more popular than the canals as they were quicker and more cost effective.

Saltaire, 1909

Saltaire was the brainchild of Titus Salt (1803–1876), the paternalistic industrialist who wanted to build a model industrial village. The village became a structure for working people around his factory and encompassed chapels and schools. The village was built between 1851 and 1872 and offered all that was thought necessary for a useful Victorian working life.

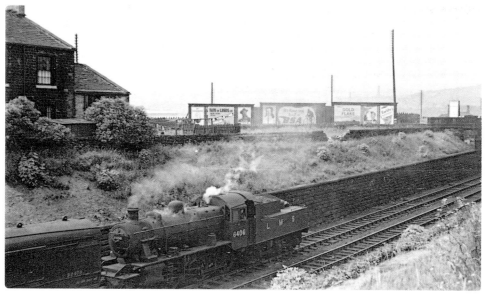

Farnley Carriage Sheds, 1947

Tram Accident, 1905

Tram accidents seemed to happen quite frequently. This one occurred on June 6th, 1905. The first attempt to gain legal permission for a tramway in London in 1857 was unsuccessful but in 1860, an American G.F. Train, opened a line in Birkenhead and three lines in London. Horsecar lines were replaced by the trams during the 1890s and this work continued for the first two decades of the 20th century. By 1908 approximately 2,500 miles of line were in operation throughout the country.

York's New Electric Car by the Mount. c. 1911

Because of its geographical location York has had a good transportation network. York lies at the junction of the rivers Ouse and Foss and in the medieval period York became an important inland port. During the 18th century it became a fashionable resort because it was on an important coaching route and the 19th century saw the rise of the commercial York, mainly due to George Hudson the "railway king" who developed it as a railway centre.

Tram Accident, Leeds. c. 1912

Interested onlookers watching this tram accident. The tramways
began to decline with the introduction of the bus and in the 1830s
with the use of the larger double-deck bus the substitution continued
at a greater pace. By the 1950s it was evident that apart from one or
two exceptions all tramlines would be gone within a few years.

Baiting the Lines at Staithes. c. 1914

Preparing the lines for fishing. Staithes is mainly famous for playing host to the grocer's shop where James Cook was apprenticed. He later became attracted to a sea-faring career and sailed from nearby Whitby to Australia.

It was thought earlier this century that many of the locals of Staithes were blue-eyed and fair-skinned with Scandinavian origins. The little-known area still possesses quaintness and a picturesque quality with its seaside character. The railways connected to Staithes but it remained relatively untouched compared to the fashionable resorts.

The River Ouse, York. c. 1904

A rather busy looking river, with numerous boats and horses and
carts. The rivers were still used for transporting goods at this time;
now the Ouse seems mainly to contain pleasure trippers.

The Tyre Shop, York. c. 1924

In the 1920s there were still a number of shops specialising in one product. This tyre shop contained motor cycle tyres, retreads, etc.

Robert Airey & Son, Huddersfield. c. 1917

The workforce gathered outside. Huddersfield was an important manufacturing town which benefited from the introduction of machinery, steam and electricity. Its ancient origins are often forgotten – it is open to debate whether Huddersfield was once a Roman station. The town grew when the canals linked the town to the seaports on both coasts, and cloth was its major product.

Copper Nob

The National Railway Museum is the home of Copper Nob which
was constructed for the Furness Railway in 1846, was withdrawn
from service in 1898 and at that time was thought to be the oldest
locomotive at work in the world.
(*A National Railway Museum Photograph.*)

Fryston Colliery, Castleford, (1972)

Castleford is situated to the southeast of Leeds and is also an area for coal mining. Industry in Yorkshire is aided by the main road and rail routes from London to northeastern England and Scotland. Another quite modern picture here shows a steam engine at work. Steam engines were used quite extensively in the coal industry.
(Photograph copyright:- Tom Heavyside)

Landing a Blue Whale, c.1918

Since medieval times herring fishing has formed the stable industry
in Whitby, although whale fishing began in 1753. Whales provided
food and oil and they have long been hunted for one or both of these.
There was also a demand for whalebone, which was used to
manufacture brushes between World War I and II and also used in
the 1950s in the corset industry.

Markham Main Colliery, Armthorpe, Nr. Doncaster, (1974)

Doncaster is known for its extensive agricultural trade and the town has large markets, although coal working is a bigger industry. Wire ropes, fencing, brass tubes, electrical equipment, agricultural machinery, clothing, nylon and confectionery are also manufactured here. Quite a modern picture here showing a steam engine busy shunting empty wagons.
(Photograph copyright:- Tom Heavyside)

Skipton Market, c.1904

North Yorkshire is an agricultural area and the North Yorkshire town of Skipton is the setting for this cattle market. The market could be an important and regular event for the farmer, for selling and buying livestock and other supplies. Farming is a complex business and efficient operation requires many skills and a lot of judgement on the part of the farmer. Factors that have an important influence are its efficiency in livestock production, prices at which products are sold, the choice of crops and effective use of labour and machinery.

Glasshoughton Coking Plant, Castleford, (1974)

An interesting scene here from not too long ago. Coal has long since been the principal product, and the Yorkshire coal measures are worked chiefly in the southwestern part of the county. To modern civilization there has been no other substance in nature except air, soil and water, so important as coal.
(Photograph copyright:- Tom Heavyside)